# BODY IMAGE
# IN THE MEDIA

GLOBAL CITIZENS: MODERN MEDIA

Published in the United States of America by Cherry Lake Publishing
Ann Arbor, Michigan
www.cherrylakepublishing.com

Content Adviser: Jessica Haag, MA, Communication and Media Studies
Reading Adviser: Cecilia Minden, PhD, Literacy expert and children's author

Photo Credits: ©Belish/Shutterstock.com, Cover, 1; ©Andrea Izzotti/Shutterstock.com, 5; ©Timur Kulgarin/
Shutterstock.com, 6; ©Everett–Art/Shutterstock.com, 7; ©chippix/Shutterstock.com, 8; ©Victorian Traditions/
Shutterstock.com, 9; ©Kari Santala/Lehtikuva/Wikimedia Commons, 10; ©milatas/Shutterstock.com, 13;
©Body Stock/Shutterstock.com, 14; ©Blend Images/Shutterstock.com, 15; ©N1_5.6/Shutterstock.com, 16;
©DONOT6_STUDIO/Shutterstock.com, 19; ©silverkblackstock/Shutterstock.com, 20; ©Dragon Images/
Shutterstock.com, 21; ©Syda Productions/Shutterstock.com, 22; ©seamind224/Shutterstock.com, 23;
©SeventyFour/Shutterstock.com, 24; ©LightField Studios/Shutterstock.com, 27; ©Stock Rocket/
Shutterstock.com, 28

Library of Congress Cataloging-in-Publication Data has been filed and is available at catalog.loc.gov

Cherry Lake Publishing would like to acknowledge the work of the Partnership for 21st Century Learning.
Please visit *www.p21.org* for more information.

Printed in the United States of America
Corporate Graphics

# ABOUT THE AUTHOR

Wil Mara has been an author for over 30 years and has written more than 100 educational titles
for children. His books have been translated into more than a dozen languages and won numerous
awards. He also sits on the executive committee for the New Jersey affiliate of the United States
Library of Congress. You can find out more about Wil and his work at www.wilmara.com.

# TABLE OF CONTENTS

# CHAPTER 1

# History: How We've Seen Ourselves

**P**eople have been communicating with each other for thousands of years. What began as rock carvings has slowly changed into books, newspapers, magazines, movies, radio, TV, and the Internet. Together, they are called **media**.

These media outlets have a powerful effect on how people see themselves. Movies, **advertisements** in magazines, commercials on television, and even books all affect a person's **body image**.

Although commonly depicted as slender, pharaohs and queens of ancient Egypt were often overweight.

## In the Ancient World

In ancient Egypt (3100–332 BCE), slender women were considered beautiful. But not all ancient societies thought that way. Ancient Greece (800–500 BCE) put greater importance on women who were heavy. Women who were too skinny were considered ill or underfed. Greek society favored men with broad shoulders, bulging muscles, and strong facial features. These features made them look like heroes. The ideal body for ancient Egyptian men was similar. The best male bodies were depicted to have broad shoulders, a narrow waist, and a clean-shaven face.

Women featured in Renaissance art were often represented as being heavier.

## An Image of Wealth

During the **Renaissance** (1300–1700 CE) in Europe, heavyset people were considered to have the ideal body. At the time, **famine** was common. So people who were heavier were thought to be healthy and rich. In the early 20th century, Americans walked less as cars became more common. Heavier people during this time were considered wealthy as well. Weight in a woman meant she was beautiful and **fertile**. Weight in a man meant he was powerful.

Many historians agree that Renaissance paintings of women were the men's way of publicly displaying their family's power and wealth.

"Strongman" circus performers were extremely popular during the late 1800s, which pressured men to become stronger and more muscular.

This attitude existed in other parts of the world as well. In Nigeria, the more weight a woman carried, the more likely she was to be chosen for marriage.

## Modern Body Image

Around the 1910s, the ideal female body was represented largely by a fictional figure known as a Gibson girl. The Gibson girl was tall, thin, fragile, and had delicate features and an impossibly narrow waist. She was depicted as **obedient** and dependent on her husband. As the media industry grew,

Women in the early 1900s wore corsets to achieve the unachievable Gibson girl look.

During the 1960s, stick-thin, boyish bodies started to gain popularity among women.

its influence on the public grew as well. The Gibson girl popped up all over the country, from advertisements in newspapers to photographs in magazines. The concept of "skinny is better" became deeply rooted in society.

In the 1920s, Coco Chanel challenged the idea that women were weak and dependent on men. She popularized an image called *garçonne*, the French word for "boy." This image paved the way for the "flapper." This girl was independent and outspoken. A flapper girl was the opposite of a Gibson girl.

Today, the Internet and social media strongly influence our standards of beauty. It is not hard to find beauty video blogs (vlogs) on YouTube and "**fitspiration**" posts on Instagram. These postings influence people's body image. For instance, a 2015 study found that women were more unhappy with their bodies after looking at fitness-inspired posts on Instagram. Men are also affected by social media. According to a study, one in three men feel pressured to look their best on social media. About 46 percent of men who take selfies take multiple shots before posting on social media.

## Developing Questions

*From this chapter, we've seen standards of beauty dramatically change from one decade to the next. For example, during times of hunger, being overweight was considered ideal. What do you think today's media and culture are saying about the ideal body? What examples can you find in movies, books, magazines, and social media that support your answer? Do you think this standard of beauty will change? Why or why not?*

# Geography: Body Image Around the World

Today's media has tremendous influence over the global population. What people see and hear through newspapers, television, and the Internet form at least part of their view of the world. The media has become so powerful that it not only reports on trends but often sets them.

## Women in Hong Kong

Being thin is valued in Hong Kong's culture. A survey found that about 36 percent of its residents ages 10 to 29 engaged in some form of weight-reduction activity. According to the

Women in Japan pay money to make their teeth crooked.
This practice is known as "yaeba."

Hong Kong **Eating Disorder** Association, in 2012 about 10 percent of women who were on **diets** to lose weight were actually underweight. A recent study also found that nearly 45 percent of young Chinese women were at risk of developing an eating disorder. Many experts blame the growing influence of the media. In youth magazines, about 20 percent of the pages are dedicated to advertisements. Of these advertisements, over 80 percent promote clothing, makeup, personal care, skin care, and slimming products!

Whey protein is consumed in order to help bulk up.
Europe is the second largest whey-protein market in the world.

## Boys in the UK

Similar to the women in Hong Kong, young men in the United Kingdom struggle with their body image. Dieting isn't the only problem for them. There's also the issue of **steroid** use in order to achieve the so-called perfect look. A study found that an additional 19,000 young men used steroids in 2017 than in 2016. Another study found that 56 percent of those who use steroids do so to look a certain way. Experts blame social media, reality television, and magazines that push a certain look. Studies have shown that young people look to social and **mainstream**

[ 21ST CENTURY SKILLS LIBRARY ]

Iran is one of the top countries that perform cosmetic nose surgeries for its men and women. Experts blame TV for the cosmetic surgery trend.

Many men in South Korea discreetly wear
high-heeled shoes in order to look taller.

media as their reference for how to look. By frequently featuring
extremely muscular men, these outlets make this look seem
normal. In reality, it is not.

## Skin-Whitening Products in Asia

People in Asia value pale skin. This standard of beauty
developed long ago. Those with darker skin were considered low
class and poor. This was because they spent most of their time
working under the sun, while those with money stayed indoors.
Pale skin is such a big part of the Asian culture that it can affect

how much you will earn, who you will marry, and what types of jobs you can get.

In Taiwan, more than 50 percent of women pay to lighten their skin. About 4 in 10 women in Hong Kong, the Philippines, South Korea, and Malaysia use some form of skin-whitening product. The pressure to do this comes from advertisements in magazines, on commercials, and even from celebrities. One popular movie star in India was featured in a skin-whitening ad. It promoted the idea that success in life and love comes from having lighter skin.

## Gathering and Evaluating Sources

The pressure to look and act a certain way is all around us—from friends to social media to movies. Look at fitness-inspired posts on social media and compare them to advertisements you see in magazines. Compare them to fitness commercials you see on television. How do these sources promote fitness and body image? Why do you think these sources pressure people to look or act a certain way? Using the Internet and your library, determine what type of media is the most powerful in influencing behavior.

# Civics: Body Image Laws

Most people will be self-conscious about their body image at some point in their lives. One reason is because so many advertisements emphasize thinness—especially fashion ads. Studies have shown that seeing the bodies of fashion models affects people's concept of ideal weight. Because of this, some countries and businesses have passed laws and rules to help reduce the pressure.

## Photoshop Laws

In 2002, about 5 percent of the youth in Israel had an eating disorder. About 90 percent of them were young women, some as young as 12 years old! Young people there continued to battle

According to studies, by the age of 10 years old, 22 percent of boys say their body image is what they worry about the most.

By the time a girl is 17 years old, she will have watched 250,000 commercials that pressure her to have an unachievable body size.

some form of eating disorder. So in 2013, Israel passed a law about images in advertising. The law requires all **Photoshopped** images to have a warning that states they have been digitally altered. It also requires that all models featured in the image have a certain **body mass index** (BMI). These models have to provide medical proof that they are within the healthy BMI range.

ModCloth, an online retailer, was the first fashion company to sign a pledge promising to not digitally alter its models' physical features.

In a UK survey, 15 percent of 18- to 24-year-old women believed that the Photoshopped images of models were accurate representations of what those women looked like in person.

Research demonstrates that one in four men may have an eating disorder. Many believe pressure from the media is to blame.

## Stock Photography

**Stock photography** is often used in print and online advertisements. Getty Images, a U.S. stock photo agency, is also taking steps to promote a healthier body image. As of October 2017, the company will no longer accept images that digitally alter the shape of a model's body. This includes retouched images that make a model look thinner or larger.

The Child Performers Protection Act of 2015 was passed in the United States to protect underage models.

## Walking the Runway

Fashion shows are held in big cities to introduce a company's new clothing line. Models wearing these clothes will walk the **runway** during the show. But in 2006, two models suffering from an eating disorder died. After that, several countries banned underweight models from walking the runway. As of 2017, four countries—Spain, Italy, France, and Israel—have adopted laws to help fight underweight modeling.

Spain was the first country to enforce the ban. It forbids extremely thin models from walking in any fashion show in Madrid. Italy also banned severely thin models from its Milan fashion shows. In France, fashion agencies and businesses can be fined more than $82,000 or go to jail for up to 6 months if they don't comply with the law. Israel has also banned underweight models from being featured in advertisements and on the runway.

## Developing Claims and Using Evidence

*People have different opinions on the use of Photoshop. Some say it enhances the image. Others say it **distorts** the image. Israel adopted a law that requires any Photoshopped image to state that it has been digitally altered. The United States does not have laws that require this, although one has been proposed. It's called the Truth in Advertising Act of 2016. Do some research using the Internet and your library. Can you find evidence for and against laws like the one in Israel and the one proposed by the United States? Using evidence you find, form your own opinion.*

# Economics: Body Image Is Big Business

The beauty industry is a $445 billion market for a reason. It profits from people's vulnerabilities. There are hundreds of products and services that promote solutions to a number of these body image issues.

## Social Media Influencers

What started out as a way to connect with friends and family has evolved into a money-making industry. Social media employs a form of marketing that uses people called influencers. Influencers have a large following on social media and have the ability to persuade their followers to buy or use a certain product. Companies pay these influencers to promote their products or services.

In 2016, the beauty industry made about $84 billion in the United States alone.

An Instagram influencer who has more than 7 million followers can potentially make over $150,000 for every promoted post. This number is doubled for YouTube accounts with more than 7 million followers. These influencers can average $300,000 for every promoted post. The promoted posts that earn the most money are generally fitness- or beauty-related.

However, getting paid to post may come with a heavier price tag. Essena O'Neill, an Australian model, used to be an influencer. She had more than 760,000 followers on Instagram, YouTube, Tumblr, and Snapchat. Despite making money for almost every

Because beauty vlogging is quickly becoming a large industry, YouTube is partnering up with L'Oréal Paris to launch an online beauty school.

post, she quit social media because it was affecting her mental health. She wanted girls to know that "social media is not real life."

## Taking Informed Action

*Everyone struggles with body image. The media knows this. It counts on these insecurities in order to make money. But that doesn't mean you should let it. Using the Internet or your library, research the different types of fashion and health ads. Do you notice more ads targeting things that women "should" fix about themselves? Do the ads target more women than men? Why do you think this is? The next time you come across an advertisement, stop and think about how it makes you feel. Does it make you feel good or bad about yourself? Think about what in the ad made you feel that way.*

# Banking on Insecurities

The fashion and beauty industries earn billions every year off people's insecurities. The nail polish industry generated about $150,000 in 1916. Four years later, that number grew to $2 million! This happened because of advertisements that warned women about how embarrassing unpolished nails were. By 2012, the industry had grown to $768 million in the United States alone.

This trend also holds true for hair dyes. During the 1950s, only about 7 percent of women dyed their hair. This changed after Clairol, a hair dye company, aggressively marketed its products. Clairol ads featured sayings like "Hate that gray? Wash it away!" Within 6 years, the company had influenced almost 50 percent of all adult women to dye their hair. According to a 2012 report, about 90 million women in the United States dye their hair.

## Communicating Conclusions

*Before you read this book, did you know that the media could affect how we think about ourselves? Now that you know more about how it can affect our body image, why do you think it's important to learn about it? Share what you've learned with your friends and family. Ask them how aware they are of the media affecting their body image.*

# Think About It

The media affects body image in boys too. A superhero costume for an 8-year-old boy often has built-in six-pack abs. Action figure toys have unrealistic and exaggerated measurements. The pressure to look a certain way is found everywhere, from video games to movies to social media.

While the media pressures women to shed weight, men are pressured to gain big muscles. In a survey of boys 8 to 18 years old, 53 percent felt they had to look a certain way because of ads. A separate study found that 69 percent of teenage boys want to have a muscular body. To gain that ideal body, 10 percent of those boys said they would take steroids while 12 percent said they would undergo surgery.

Knowing that the media affects body image for both boys and girls, what do you think can be done to reduce this pressure? Would more body diversity in movies, magazines, and television help? Why or why not? What about more ads that portray positive messages about our bodies? Research different ways the media can positively impact body image. Research different ways you can stay positive about your own body image.

# For More Information

## Further Reading

Albers, Susan. *Eating Mindfully for Teens: A Workbook to Help You Make Healthy Choices, End Emotional Eating, and Feel Great.* Oakland, CA: New Harbinger Publications, 2018.

Kilpatrick, Haley, and Whitney Joiner. *The Drama Years: Real Girls Talk About Surviving Middle School—Bullies, Brands, Body Image, and More.* New York: Free Press, 2012.

Rissman, Rebecca. *Asking Questions About Body Image in Advertising.* Ann Arbor, MI: Cherry Lake Publishing, 2016.

## Websites

**KidsHealth—Body Mass Index**
http://kidshealth.org/en/kids/bmi.html?WT.ac=ctg#catfit
Learn more about your BMI and how to stay healthy.

**KidsHealth—Kids and Eating Disorders**
https://kidshealth.org/en/kids/eatdisorder.html#catfit
Discover how unhealthy eating habits can become dangerous.

**Kids Helpline—How to Be Happy Being Yourself**
https://kidshelpline.com.au/kids/issues/how-be-happy-being-yourself
Read about how to appreciate who you are.

# GLOSSARY

**advertisements** (AD-vur-tize-muhnts) broadcast or published notices that call attention to something, such as a product or an event

**body image** (BAH-dee IM-ij) the way a person views their physical self

**body mass index** (BAH-dee MAS IN-deks) a measurement that shows the amount of fat in your body and that is based on your weight and height

**diets** (DYE-its) food plans that limit the amount a person eats in order to help reduce weight

**distorts** (dih-STORTS) twists out of the normal condition in order to mislead someone

**eating disorder** (EET-ing dis-OR-dur) any of several illnesses marked by abnormal eating behaviors

**famine** (FAM-in) an extreme shortage of food

**fertile** (FUR-tuhl) able to have babies

**fitspiration** (fits-puh-RAY-shuhn) a person or thing that serves as motivation for someone to improve their health and fitness

**mainstream** (MAYN-streem) ideas or activities thought to be normal or typical

**media** (ME-dee-uh) a method of communication between people, such as a newspaper

**obedient** (oh-BEE-dee-uhnt) doing what you are told

**Photoshopped** (FOH-toh-shahpd) to change a picture using image-editing software, such as Photoshop, in a way that distorts reality

**Renaissance** (REN-uh-sahns) the period of European history between the 14th and 17th centuries marked by a flourishing of art and literature inspired by ancient times and by the beginnings of modern science

**runway** (RUHN-way) a raised walkway that extends from a stage into the audience, used in fashion shows

**steroid** (STER-oid) a chemical substance used to increase muscle size and strength but that may have harmful effects

**stock photography** (STAHK fuh-TAH-gruh-fee) pictures of common places, nature, or people that, for a fee, can be used and reused for commercial purposes

# INDEX